PADLA

Breakfast of the Magi

BREAKFAST OF THE MAGI

J. LIVINGSTONE CLARK

Thistledown Press Ltd.

©John Livingstone Clark, 1994
All rights reserved

Canadian Cataloguing in Publication Data

Clark, R.J. (Ronald John), 1950-
  Breakfast of the magi / John L. Clark. —
  Poems.
  ISBN 1-895449-25-1
PS8555.L37185B7 1994   C811'.54   C94-920071-9
PR9199.3.C437B7 1994

Book design by A.M. Forrie
Cover painting by Miranda Jones
Typeset in 11pt. New Baskerville by Thistledown Press Ltd.

Printed in Canada by
Hignell Printing Ltd.
Winnipeg, Manitoba

Thistledown Press Ltd.
633 Main Street
Saskatoon, saskatchewan
S7H 0J8

Acknowledgements:
The author wishes to thank the Saskatchewan Arts Board for their support, Anne
Szumigalski for her editorial assistance and George McWhirter for his
encouragement.
Some of the poems in this book have appeared in *Grain*, *NeWest Review* , *Prairie
Fire* and *Towards 2000: Poetry For The Future.*

This book has been published with the assistance of The Canada Council and the
Saskatchewan Arts Board.

for Helen Jean and Robert Edgar

CONTENTS

1. THE BREAKFAST OF THE MAGI

EXTINCTION ODE: FOR PANSIES   10

DEAD POET TURNS MIND SOUTH   11

THE BRIGHT WORDS   12

THE BREAKFAST OF THE MAGI   13

MARTHA'S OLD GALS   14

EPIPHANY, SEPTEMBER 1991   15

EGG PERFECTION   16

EPIPHANY, OCTOBER 1991: THE ECTASY FACTOR   17

LUCRETIA'S *CRI DE COEUR* ON C.B.C.   18

WINTER MEDITATION   19

PENMANSHIP AND SALVATION   20

THE POET AND FRIENDS (1)   21

CRYPTO EROTICA   22

UNTITLED ASCENT   23

COOL RESPITE IN WHITE   24

TO DAPHNE WITH HER GLOVES OFF   25

TEARY INTERROGATIONS   26

AXIS MUNDI /descent   27

THE ROUND OF LOVE   28

MY LOVE'S DOMAIN   29

QUIET GREEN BLANKETS   30

THE POESYCEPHALIC AT REST   31

THE POET AND FRIENDS (2)   32

THE POET AND FRIENDS (3)   33

A LOVE DEFINED   34

FLIGHT PLANS   35

THE PARABOLIC PLAIN   36

2. EATING FROM THE OCEAN

WEST/ GEIST   39

THE RIGHT CUT FOR CASH   40

THE MARTYRED BUGS   41

THE KIDS ON FIRE   42

SEX TALKING   43

AGAINST LOVE AND THE ANT/ THROPOCENTRIC   44

EXISTENTIAL BREAKFAST   46

THE ETIQUETTE OF EATING FROM THE OCEAN   47

ORANGE JUICE EPIPHANY   48

THE WOMAN WITH MOLTEN WORDS   50

THE REAL WOMAN, FRANCIS   51

JACK'S CAFE/ EAST END/ 22 APRIL 1990   52

HOUSE HUBBY FEVER   54

FOR SWEETEST BETSY   56

DULCE (this dulse) *ET DECORUM*   57

FOR CHRISTINE THE JAZZ GROUPIE I LOVED   58

NOVENA FOR GRACE KELLY   59

3. FROM THE CAULDRON

FROM THE ABYSMAL CAULDRON   61

SO FRIGGIN' BLUE   62

DIAPHANEITY, THE VISIBLE ORIGINS   63

FROGS AND WASPS   64

OREGON RAIN   65

THE POET AND FRIENDS (4)   66

ANIKO/ ONE   67

ANIKO/ TWO   69

ANIKO/ THREE   70

ANIKO/ FOUR   71

THE PRACTICE OF DEPTH   72

A NEW SLANT ON EXTINCTION   73

FLIGHT   74

BEDTIME GNOSIS   75

IT IS CLEAR   76

GAVIN'S FEET: THE PERILS OF NEGATIVE THEOLOGY   77

THE FINGER STEEPLE POINTING   78

OH, THE WONDER   79

BREAKFAST OF THE MAGI

EXTINCTION ODE: FOR PANSIES   /10

From this time of language pull hymns, rhymes and nursery songs
for dinosaurs are in the dahlias and serpents are in the sun
flowers.   These are the last times, the violets seem to say,
these are the final hours for cornflowers and forget-me-nots.
And whose children are these? you thornily ask. They're yours
and mine, for all children belong even these orchids and
daisies.

All forms of light are mine! saith the Flower God,
even fleabane and the vaginal rose called carnation. But the
big scaly feet of the terrible lizards trample all the dream
gardens and make the kids scream! No wonder they suffer from
terminal nightmares, no wonder they sleep at their desks during
class.   What's this bullshit, you say, they're only flowers!
But please never say only flowers, for the water lily once
was your mother's placenta — the Nymphaea fruit you feed on
at night.

DEAD POET TURNS MIND SOUTH /11

Will the tomatoes ripen in time?
Green and heavy
they hang from their vines
on the concrete wall at my window.

In this country
winter begins in August
and poetry
means less than rodeo.
What survives
is simply what survives.
Words mean nothing more
than what they mean,
and that seems paltry little.

But somewhere there is more light
and warmth   where things can ripen
from green to gold.
A thought could do it, or a poem.
Somewhere south in the open.

THE BRIGHT WORDS

She loves the words I love,
Epiphany, ineffable.
So I proffer the grace
Of the adjectival form —

Aaahh, *epiphanic!* And
We marvel how it haloes
Simple things on the ground.

Yes, gardens intrigue me —
Your careful bright words.

THE BREAKFAST OF THE MAGI   /13

Only hours before you gave birth we had breakfast
with Liz at that place on the river. Seated near the
big windows, you were the first to see that mallard
with the peculiar head. How much like a dinosaur, you
commented, leaning serenely on the table. Liz con-
curred, calling all birds *dinosaurish,* while I
ordered bacon and extra toast. Our sexual procliv-
ities vary from year to year, but we are totally
in agreement on this basic issue: sex is not the
most basic issue. Even with one of us bulging at
the seams, a ripe pink pod, we three are Magi
of the Imagination. Slipping through a gate at
the back of the mind — down a long summer trail —
going far and golden beyond the walls.

MARTHA'S OLD GALS /14

Martha's old gals give her more love than
almost anyone.   Mrs. Mitchell, for example,
said one day, while looking out the window,
It's only one sky — yet it rains
here and there.

Mrs. Buchan, on the other hand, said this
about leaving the sprinklers on: *If you*
keep them on long enough   first the canaries
will come   then the bird of paradise.
It's nice that these frail old blossoms
need her so much   and love her so long,
for we both despair of the times and the
colour of the planet's aura.   She quotes
as often as she can the following lines:
Whether the shadow becomes our friend or
enemy   depends largely upon ourselves.

In a dry summer, though, it's the sprinkler
that really matters   for shadows run like
ink when the earth turns to rain.   There's
only one sky, we pause to remember   then
come canaries   and the bird of paradise.

EPIPHANY, SEPTEMBER 1991 /15

Thunderheads boil in from Rosetown
and the multifoliate sky
blossoms forth forms unseen
in a sacristy of silence.
There's not an idea left
that can transverse the span
of the great *IS,* I think.
But heavy rains for May,
even some snow,   and those
greens are richer than ever.

First a time of green — then a
longer time of brown, or yellow-
burnt almond — then finally
white. Purity like a colour
to put you to sleep.

EGG PERFECTION

/16

I love you and you love me and though Stalin butchered
millions, he sprang from the egg as surely as you and I.

And what can we do about it? Pray to Jesus? He sprang
from the egg and right onto a tree: nailed, mocked, slain.

I love me and you love you and though Jesus loved the masses,
He sprang from the egg as surely as you and I —

And what's to be done about it? Nothing. For the egg
holds the center in its perfect whiteness.

EPIPHANY, OCTOBER 1991: THE ECSTASY FACTOR /17

Tonight my Born Again friends will arrive from Hannah,
Alberta. I was like the man beaten and near death in the
wilds; they were like the good Samaritan — Mr. and Mrs.
Bruce Samaritan, of no fixed address in this world. I'm
no longer of their Faith, at least not to the outer eye,
so how will I fix them breakfast, how will I position
their beds? To me they belong in a nursery, and I'm sure
they see me sizzling like bacon in a pan — still, we
all acknowledge the primacy of light.

Meanwhile, across the common, a redheaded woman lunches
while watching over some school kids. I know her a
little — she is beautiful and eats cookies with more grace
and delicacy than I. Yet here I sit contented with my
burgeoning thoughts — that jazz of the divine
setting sweet reeds to singing.

LUCRETIA'S *CRI DE COEUR* ON C.B.C.

I park and sit quietly watching the river
while the steady hum of hospital generators,
the airliners roaring overhead,
are like mechanized mantras leading nowhere.
Still,   spring is spring,
and even Lucretia's plangent lament
can't steal simple joy
from the geese honking north.

WINTER MEDITATION

The winter roars its wrath through the sheet metal veins
of this small old house, and I feel winter in my feet
leeching up from the floor. Poems like blossoms fall
silently onto the pages of books and are pressed inward
to seal their fragile beauty; and when all flowers have
fallen from the sky, there are still branches that lean
up into heaven.

Like frail Schoolmen, with sharp tongues and finely
tuned ratios, these dark silhouettes wait solemnly
for the flame. But winter will take them as well, rising
through the trunk, engirding the heart with silence.
There, too, sleep will stay — blossoms gone, branches
still, roots thrust deep in dreaming earth. Poems
long-fingered like ancient lore,   quiet
as the final page.

PENMANSHIP AND SALVATION   /20

Mrs. Hunt! Thank you for those hard hours sweating
over McLean Method of Penmanship. No one could
make mandalas like you on the board, cosmic pies
hurtling across the dark green sky. On Fridays
we'd use coloured chalk, like carnival time, but
you kept us on our sacred path: circles, ovals,
loops, spirals — all that we might do ourselves
proud in the reticular eyes of Mr. McLean . . .

Today Mrs. Hunt, years after you drove your
white Falcon coupe straight to heaven — today,
with Mater Matter writhing under Man's malevolent
touch — today Mistress Hunt, dear Athena of the
Ink Wells, I make circles in your honour.
Perfect rings to heal my hands:
Imago Terra Nova.

THE POET AND FRIENDS (1)   /21

The bamboo screen around my desk
is clean, dry and golden, he said calmly.
And when I'm finished for the night
it rolls up nicely like a quiver
for my loves: two perfect circles
and a world strung between —
one looking outward, the other
within.

CRYPTO EROTICA /22

So we don't make love anymore, who's the worse
for wear? Besides, when you finally write a book
you'll make royalties enough to float us both
across the Pacific. Aahhh, sonorous, sibilant
Gauguin — all the best words begin with 's':
salacious, salubrious, sanguineous, sexy.
So simple satyrs samba on the sea-shore, and
coffee coloured maidens lean naked over my
hammock. This is the life, warm, bountiful:
even our beautiful Lord might have taken His
time down here beneath gentler palms. No
rush to the cross, no frozen northern angst.

We don't make love anymore and so both dream
of light on a far blue sea. Distance raised
to virtue, what kind God still smiles on us?

UNTITLED ASCENT

/23

When you're dreaming and asleep, I know
candles appear on mahogany tables.   Also,
roses in crystal and lovers by the peck.
They are always otherworldly, or like
no one you've ever known.   Are they
your future?   I hope so.

You've earned a little tenderness,
your decanter always dry.   And when
demons come at night, pulling softly
at my nipples   you're safely away
dream dancing.   Perhaps
someday soon
I'll climb up to your need.

COOL RESPITE IN WHITE /24

Lifting her face one day
To me and the world,
The curve of her neck
Caught a plenitude of beauty,

And for a moment out of time
The dying animal froze,
Looking out the window,
Passing muster on the roses,

While I froze with her,
Love giving such solace,
Cool respite in white
From the grim quick times.

TO DAPHNE WITH HER GLOVES OFF

Love, I give you one
more chance — take the
tape from my ribs,
the casts from my
fists. Love, the
swelling around my
eyes has subsided,
and the green shines
through, emerald and
fine. Love, in your
many incarnations
you have won all the
matches. But the
beatings get milder
each time.

TEARY INTERROGATIONS   /26

It's Daphne's weepy morning as magpies
puddle carouse — Nothing sacred! Nothing
sacred!   their corvine cackles infer.
And she weeps on afternoonish
till something comes on radio-wise:
light   buoyant   bubbly.

Why so much pain in the world?
she inquires the wireless.   Where's
God's Love   or a real good time?
Meanwhile, pigeons roam in hot
August sunspell, the smell of
cedars everywhere, the moan
of ornamentals dying   even dog
shit on the restless, ragged lawn.

But Daphne weeps till the crows
go home   leaves grass uncut.
Just smokes by the door.

AXIS MUNDI /descent   /27

We argue now more than ever,
take liberties with speech,
cut, parry, thrust —
go to bed molten with rage,
never touch, never kiss.

If the very Lord of Heaven
were to slip between us now
nothing would change
I think — just less room
on the pillows and something
more to bitch about:
Who's he, your cousin?
Tell 'im to push off!

THE ROUND OF LOVE /28

He loved her and I loved her and someone else once loved her
and who does she love? Woman, thy name is whispered in the
court of the rose; thy name is Temptress, also Mother, Sister,
Nun and Whore. He once loved her but she threw him over, then
I loved her for awhile but she tired of my wheezing. Waltzes
are beautiful things, she said, but you can turn them into
endurance contests. She now loves someone else, though still
loving me in a special way — I love you, she says, but I'm
not IN love with you. I thank her for those meager crumbs, I
thank her for letting me phone on Sunday afternoons — she is
awake by then, usually, has showered, and is lying on cushions
with a view of both sea and mountains. Avoid caviar, she
advises, you know how it gives you gas. I take her counsel,
seriously too, for I'm IN love with another who'll maybe
love me — we'll see.

MY LOVE'S DOMAIN   /29

A life turned this way and that by love.
There are worthier domains, perhaps —
there is the mind, with its calculus
and falling apples.   There are the senses,
Monsieur De Sade and his playful ways.

There is also the life of action, com-
bining all of the above.   But this
is mine, the way of Love and its
painful turning. Lavender light
in the body's hollows.

QUIET GREEN BLANKETS   /30

Not a small man, curled in damp green woolen blankets
but light, as though fever had left a transparency.
For deliriums come and if not fatal go — bodies mend
and minds.   Blankets can be aired. And rooms? A bou-
quet of flowers (roses, carnations) can do wonders
erasing the memories of illness.

A big man lying asleep in his bed, curled up tight
in heavy green counterpanes: a wedding gift from
parents decades before.   Two lovely green blankets of
spring, though he's been alone for years and their
colour now faded.   Also, dust everywhere, the large
man's breathing now quick and shallow like hidden
bellows. And in summer's heat the sweet green hills
soon damp with sweat, the man's thick curly hair
growing wild on the pillows.

THE POESYCEPHALIC AT REST

In bed with arms, legs and all the rest set to wander
the labyrinth of dreams, I search quietly for perfect
words, intoning strange new syllables from the mammal
arcanum. What roses will rise from their thorny graves
to greet me? What gnosis will rise like a giant squid
to pull me down to my final rapture?   All is lost
where the Word is found too quickly.

THE POET AND FRIENDS (2)   /32

With a mop of wild hair, pants tucked into socks
bookbag balanced on his made-from-scratch bike
you wouldn't take him for a Romantic — for a
sensuous soul.   But he is — beneath a ton
of glib learning, his heart's like a marvelous
nude, all covered with hats and yellow
raincoats.   And every once in a while he'll
fall off his wheels:
words combing the mud for a real presence,
nude blinking back tears in the common light.

THE POET AND FRIENDS (3)   /33

Your poems are never simple enough, she said
easing his arm from her shoulder —
why can't you write like this guy?   Here
this one's beautiful: someone slept
with his wife, his best friend in fact,
and someone else cut off their foot.
See?   The stitches are so real
they make you shiver with the needle.
Your stuff makes me dizzy — and
when you read them, all you want is
approval.   If I say what I think
you just hit the roof.

OK, he said, you're right — I'm
a bad tempered prick with a fiery tongue.
With your crinoline wings all scorched
and black, how will you ever fly?
Never, she said, I never will —
but the weight of your head on the
base of my spine keeps me straight
on the road that I'm running.

A LOVE DEFINED /34

Love and knowledge,
two legs the journey
rides out upon —
or swims, kicking
or flies
feathers clutched
in foolish wax.
It falls
this gnostic love:
legs broken,
heart drained.

Who says these
are only words?
Who says
only pain and
bondage?
The most com-
pelling of dreams
says light
breaks forward
and up.

FLIGHT PLANS   /35

An organ concerto by Vivaldi: for a moment
the celestial order of angels' dances
along the keyboard's upper register. This
provides graceful accompaniment to wind
chimes outside in the green spring breeze.
Inside, I listen to the complaints of what I
know best: a mind tired of minding; a heart
weary of hearing; kidneys bored with kidding
around; a liver sick of living. From deep
within this husk the rapture stirs, wants to
fly the way of the soul's upper register.

THE PARABOLIC PLAIN   /36

Over the plains they come,
                    the denizens of the first order.

Walking tall, stooping once or twice for water and herbs.
These are the magicians of dawn. Stopping each hour for
prayers and cigarettes, lying down with their children
on the spring green grass.

                        Over the plains they come, down
the small river valleys to bathe at the weirs. And no one sees
them anymore. No one measures their solemn beauty against the
crippled children of time.

                        Duration has become everything in
this place. And over the plains swing the sojourners of a
timeless dawn. And no one sees them anymore, working their
intricate silver in the soft lilac light. Small hammers
beating like the heart of a poem.

                        For only poems travel
with them, embroidering the prairie with infinite design.

/37

The children are fine,   saith the plain
                         saith the earth.
The children are fine,   saith the sky
                         saith the dream.

The children are doing fine, so don't worry. The children
of the denizens of the first order.

                        Their beauty is matchless
and the inflictions of time will never enter the realms of
their solemn inclination.

                        And over the plains we follow, walking
quietly, unsure of true north or any other proposition. And
where the sun marks its absence on the lip of the earth,
there we mark our terminus. The realm of those children
and the timeless inclination.

EATING FROM THE OCEAN

And it's west again in summer, dusty and dry, while
kids in pickups roar out dirt roads, six to a cab, and
blondes pretend they're dazzled — summer in the hot,
dirty west, with farmers goin' broke, droppin' dead,
while old babushkas pray for rain at small town altars
made from spuds.   Only in the Rockies is it cool at
night   at the foot of great granite peaks where
goof bears shit on tourist sites, steal sushi, then
hide in the spruce and pine.   On the far rainy slopes
things are green only in the minds of old-timers —
Twenty years of cutting left, says the last honest
ranger, just fired. *Twenty years, then the sticks are
all gone. When the big companies pull out, it'll all
be one big ghost town! 'Cept for Vancouver, of course.
She'll be a duty free port with sweat shops making
cheap jeans for hungry starlets*   Yes, the future's
looking good for carnivores: especially the ones
with fine pelts.

THE RIGHT CUT FOR CASH   /40

So it's a grey flannel world I'm thinking about, a special kind
of world up early in the morning — showered and shaved it wears
English Leather or musky cologne. Yes! A freshly flannelled
morning, slightly belled at bottom, sharply pressed and flared,
for these trousers are like great tall ships, setting off on
secret missions. Every day they sail out like Morgan's priva-
teers — taking no prisoners, they rampage through commerce,
firing broadsides at the market . . .

Yes, forget the body, it's the cut of the trouser that leaves' em
panting. Willingly hostaged stenos in floral see-me-alls lie
back entranced by blue blazered Vikings. And in their wildest
dreams, they are swept off to tax-free Valhallas where every
night's desire awaits the surcharge of three-piece bulls — O
to be a Kaiser in those lily white fields, King of Coal, King
of Crotch. So it's a three-piece, grey flannel morning I'm
dreaming of, raising the sails on my old battered rig — left
dress, right dress, there's lucre to lay in.

THE MARTYRED BUGS   /41

Leatherjackets aren't so tough, riding blithely into any place
they want — I whap them with rolled up newspapers and they
crumble, O how they crumble — their long legs kicking like June
Taylor dancers, high-stepping to the wind's brisk rhythm — then
Whap, Whap, Whap, all the joy stripped from their merry dance,
Whap! Whap! Whap! Clinging to the walls like forgotten saviours:
O God, O God, why hast Thou forsaken us? These are the aban-
doned of all bugs. Hungry for love with their Hollywood pins, they
dream of polished hardwood floors, bright footlights, crowds
of cheering army grunts.   But now, smeared to a wall like Our
 Lord on the cross, it freaks me out — the pathos, the pathos!
And I pray for their forgiveness — pass them vinegar on sponge
and toothpick. I divide their coriaceous garments. I even stick
pins in their sides, just to make sure — no water and wine, but
signum they are, nevertheless, broken and bent, stuck to the
paradise of my white plaster wall.   Lordy, Lordy, Lordy! They
ascend into quiet while I weep for my murderous sins.

THE KIDS ON FIRE   /42

And the night progresses with a great blues band
swinging on the stand: wicked horns, wild rhythms
but best of all a youngster from black Chicago town
totally wicked on lead guitar.   Hermes! we cry from
our tables, being literary men, Hermes! what's new
with the gods?   He just smiles and I think, boy,
if this kid don't get laid tonight, there's some-
thing fundamentally wrong with this town. But he
just keeps playing every lick that's ever been
imagined, keeping Whitehead's God in mind, and that
old *infinite possibility* zaps us through lightning
bolt strings, and we're all yelling Fire, Fire, the
kids on Fire! The joint's on Fire!   And what with
all the eye-balling going on, I don't think we're
lying.   But the owner thinks we're trying to cause
a riot, which is true, being anarchists and all, so
they boot us out!   But that's OK with the bards,
cuz by now we all know the words — *little red
rooster doin' fine.*

SEX TALKING /43

This gland has taken me a long way, the wrinkled poet thought
sitting at his desk, fingering his cock — it's like a pen,
un stylo, always in reserve. And when I'm dry, when nothing
comes to the virgin page, I play with myself — I roll hairy
gourds through my fingers while dreaming of sweet white
lilies: coracle size, they sail me away to distant maiden
shores. I've had them all, you know, every colour, shape
and size, and loved them all, too — none of this white man's
burden. I've read Kraft-Ebbing and Malinowsky; rolled with
Maggie Mead, guiltless on the bodies of oiled islanders, tits
and pricks all over the place. Read and done all that stuff.
But now I just sit back behind bamboo screens, while true
love brews a fresh pot of green tea.

AGAINST LOVE AND THE ANT/THROPOCENTRIC   /44

It is April again. April of warm spring days and lilac smells.
April of lovers and other fools on public benches — but April,
sweetest month, is mostly for ants.   And they scurry about in
freshman beanies, dreaming about getting laid by the Queen: but
are also disciplined in ways human's can't even imagine.   These
small pismires can carry their weight in gold, and are stronger
by far than psychotic grannies looking for the old homestead.
But do they ever lose their cool?   Sure, they're small and so-
ciable, and who wouldn't be — living forever in the cold, dark
earth.   But what if it's different, what if the bug-geeks are
wrong? What if surfacing depresses the hell out of these hymen-
opterous hustlers?   What if the mere sight of us makes them
all want to puke?

Mankind: starched, laundered and loitering in parks; pairs in
pastels reconnoitering with their tongues — lovers, perverts.
Tee-hee, go little pupae pups, tagging along with pater for
some simple biology. "Uuhhh-hummm! Now pay attention class to
these young mammals with their big and dangerous shoes.   These
creatures are in heat, and don't ask me to explain because it's
just too darn embarrassing — you'd think their parents would
teach them something useful, like how to carry heavy loads over
endless obstacles with their mouths. But nooo! THEY'VE GOT TO
LOUNGE AROUND THIS PERFECTLY GOOD PASTURE SUCKINGTONGUE
AND DON'T ASK ME WHAT TONGUE IS!

/45

Is it like feeling someone's tentacles too long? one of the kids
asks. "Whoever told you about that?" Pop zips back, "it's a lot
worse, so don't you kids get any strange ideas — your first duty
and allegiance is to the hill, and don't you forget it! Why our
glorious Queen just bursts into tears every time one of you goes
wrong — and she knows it too, yes, she surely does! Why with
her magical powers, she knows all about the imagoes hiding down
under the steps, feeling each other's tentacles and making those
jived-up cricket sounds with their hind legs. She sheds buckets
of tears every time the hill is betrayed, and it hurts her more
than it hurts them when she sends troops to tear off their
heads to feed to the larvae. But c'mon kids, we're not here
for a picnic — you've got to pay close attention now — when
these big, bipedal carbon-units get steamed up, they start run-
ning through grass and clover, mooing like kinky quadrapeds —
and maybe they'll fall down on the green, rolling about slurp-
ing and smacking! And let me tell you, they can kill a mound
full of ants in no time at all! Why, there's nothing more
scary anywhere than a pair of humans rubbing their feelers
and making cricket sounds with their hind legs.

EXISTENTIAL BREAKFAST   /46

It isn't clear how I faced-off with mortality while
eating breakfast at the Broadway Cafe, but I did, staring
hungrily down at my poached eggs, bacon and hashbrowns.
I started thinking up a story: in it, a very old man is
asked about the key to longevity. His response? "Grease!
A good greasy plate of grub every morning — then a smoke
over the local newsrag." It seemed funny at the time,
trowelling jam on the well buttered toast, but as I de-
molished my coronary special, I could see I was gorging
in bad faith — just whistling past the urn. I'd never
see sixty, not with my lust for hot grilled ambrosia —
cholesterol was building a Great Wall around my heart,
loyalty to working class tucker like a tombstone around
my neck — without sprouts I was doomed. When the end
comes, I mused, I'll be seated at this table inhaling
fried spuds, dripping eggs and glazed ham — hashslingers
will bear my carcass on a teacart, the chef weeping at the
waste, at the ragout I might have graced.

Grief stricken and terrified I could barely stand to pay
my bill. I'm sorry, I whimpered, I don't have change for
a tip. But the waitress smiled like an angel, and just
squeezed my trembling hands — Don't worry, she said, it's
a pleasure to serve you. And there shone heaven through
pearly white teeth: a full refund guaranteed or a bromide
on the house.

THE ETIQUETTE OF EATING FROM THE OCEAN /47

When prying open the soft-shelled mollusk
warm gently by rubbing and applying
light pressure. Also, kelp and rockweed
may be hiding the lips, the portal
to the soft tasty center within.

Gently disentangle such salty wet
strands, and never thrust intrusively.
Rather, tickle lightly the mollusk's
delicate antenna, then watch it
gasp open in delight. Apply butter
and consume. Lobster bib optional.

ORANGE JUICE EPIPHANY /48

Tell me something about love and beauty, the woman at the
Orange Julius counter crooned, and I stammered and splut-
tered, helping her to a table with a big tray loaded with
food and drink. *Universals, these of course are universal
in the broadest sense ... uugghhh, and being of an abstract
and unconditional nature, participate in the realm of . . .
uuggghhhh.* And that was as far as I got. Her lips were
thin and cruel, with bright scimitar teeth glinting wicked
under perfect nose. And those eyes — were they drawn hastily
from some far flung desert sky? Was she completely human?
I wasn't sure, though she seemed precise in a cool and math-
ematical way, and I dared not risk what little I knew of
Plato and the archetypal zone.

Not that I couldn't afford lunch — even without sufficient
change I could have read her palm, sung her some plainsong,
dazzled her with obscure Celtic lore — what's a chili dog
worth these days? Calmly she took everything I had to give,
without once breaking wind or proffering an opinion: I was
intellectually eviscerated; I was left panting on my plastic
stool. Sure I deserved it — most fatuous and flatulent of
all city poets — but who's keeping score? Was she angel or
demon? Natural blonde or touched up albino?

Thank you for your wit and healthy nescience, she smiled
gently, rising without effort on calves and thighs well
muscled and tanned. *These quick, greasy lunches are so bor-
ing without company. Don't you think?* Again I stammered,
reduced to pebbles in the mouth of an ancient Greek: *Yes,
yes . . . of course, let me help you with your wrap.* It was
a line I'd learned from an old Leslie Howard movie, but
she rebuffed it like flame scorching a moth. *Please, finish
your meal. And these scraps, don't let them go to waste . . .
for me, my little carbuncle.*

And so I wailed loudly, regardless of fashion, for her power
was like that of an infinite mirror, revealing my every
fault and failure.   She was Beauty and Love to be sure,
but not of the snuggling kind.

THE WOMAN WITH MOLTEN WORDS

The woman casts her thighs through every reading
like they're made of molten steel.
Yes, I could devour you   they warn every man in the
room.   But I'll raise my skirt instead, and read
you my latest stuff.   And it's good, real good —
and all about the sexual properties of simple
numbers and fractions.   Oooohhh, the 1 gets me hot
so very, very hot — and look at the buns on
that 3, tight like a young avocado — or, I'd go
down on that 7 anytime, anywhere — but best
of all, I like the 8   real hairy on its side
it hangs and jingles like bells.

Rearranging her skirt, she curtsies   while
the crowd goes wild with sighs.   Meanwhile, an old
surveyor with a butt pasted to his lip sneers
approvingly.   *Let's go, baby*, he wheezes, *I wanna
show you the lights that sparkle the dark
on my pocket calculator.*

THE REAL WOMAN, FRANCES   /51

Frances loves the Lord and makes obeisance in
Saran Wrap when her husband comes home.   Carefully
he unwraps his jelly slicked goddess.   Mmmmnnn, he
slavers, the goodness of the grape is righteous!
And she readily nods her approval   for duty is
upon her like sugar on a doughnut, and her man
has returned from the mountain of fire, burdened
and anxious to ordain his bride.   The kids are
asleep, *God speed, kind sir* — and he's on her
with a fury, stones ready to break.

JACK'S CAFE/ EAST END/ 22 APRIL 1990   /52

The meat is good in this place
last night the beef, this morning
the best bacon I've ever tasted.
Old boys at the counter like
shiny brass spittoons.   A young
guy comes in and tells a joke:
What do farmers and 747's have in
common? Ten minutes after they land
in Hawaii, they both stop whining.
Everyone laughs for this is a
friendly place.   I laugh too, and
the Heart Sutra says: *Dwell not*
in the inner Void. Boy, am I fucked!
The soul's dark night has me firmly
by the ears, my nose buried deep
in her garden. Then: *Pursue not*
the outer entanglements.

The young Greek cook comes out to
jaw with some frisky old ladies. My
cat kept me awake all night, one
grannie steams. SHOOT IT! roars

/53

Spartan with spatula. Grannie looks
scared, producing much wind and
noise — dust devil with loose
upper plate. Oh, I like cats,
he quietly assures her — dead
cats! guffaw, guffaw, guffaw,
then back to his coleslaw

I look at my bacon.
Too crispy to be cat?
I've seen some pretty porcine
tabbies. Tough world.
Demands a stance. Like
Dwell not in inner darkness.
(We first saw this cafe
22 years ago, the trophy
heads on the wall reminisce,
but from where did we begin?
Where are we now?)

This mysterium endlessly
running — complex of gas, light
and amino acids — defeats me
and all tough stances. Just
an inner light pressing
always   and outward.

HOUSE HUBBY FEVER /54

As he diapered the boy, fed him porridge, bathed his
tender limbs, he dreamed of another life. It was filled
with beautiful bronzed animals, all long stemmed American
beauties — blondes, brunettes, red-heads with slender long
legs and smooth careful shoulders. *The House Husband*, he
thought ruefully to himself, a treatise from some myopic,
coke-bottled shrink — *The House Frigging Husband*, by Pro-
fessor Merton Rondo, a work to rival Malinowski's great
tome *Argonauts of the Western Pacific*. Quoting from the
text we might read the following: "The house husband wanders
through the few empty rooms fate has consigned to him. He is
unemployed, perhaps even terminally unemployable. Not that
fate has been completely unfair: his wife, or the woman who
passes for his wife, let's say the mother of his last son,
yes, that very woman, is gainfully employed. She brings
home the bacon, to employ a phrase not popular with porcine
folk, the very bacon he feels he should be bringing home.
Aahhh, memories of fatherhood in the great rugged north —
heavily muscled men climbing into trucks, wet October morn-
ings, sons fighting to pack the old man's gut-bucket out
to the waiting lorry, heavy thermos bottles filled with hot
java, stacks of cold beef sandwiches. Then tatooed and sun
leathered hands reaching down to pale boys: *Watch out when
I back up now, I don't wanna run over yer fucking heads.*

/55

Stopping at all school crossings, in little towns up and
down the mountainous coast, these tender thugs would whistle
softly as pretty young teachers strolled with their stumpy
charges. These brawny brutes of the woods would wink and
dream of soft white thighs and red garters *flambeau,* while
the rustle of silk stockings would throw them into perilous
reveries. Later on, out in the bush, they'd need all their
wits, what with heavy steel cables and monster chokers
flying through the air — poontang wasn't worth dying for,
or hardly ever!

So the house hubby longed for greasy diesels and tatooed
forearms. His hands smelt mostly like shit and bleach,
which wasn't the same at all: there being no masculine
pride in it. But trashing stinking disposables was hardly
death-defying work, and that freed his mind for all kinds of
dreaming. Without any fear of losing life or limb, he'd sing
softly to himself, *Swing low, sweet cherry blossom,* then
draw snakes and anchors on his arms with black ink. *Thank
heavens for lady posties,* he'd think while checking the
time . . . *especially the young stuff.*

FOR SWEETEST BETSY   /56

In 1970 Art Garfunkle sang
"Bridge Over Troubled Water"
and the guy who owned the ESSO
station in Smithers, B.C.,
fell in love with my only
friend's wife. She was lovely
bold and sexy, and once
playing spin the bottle at
a party, I kissed her
seven times in a row.
The bottle was saying,
You two are dreamy together,
and her mouth and tongue
were sweeter than honey.
But the grease-monkey
used to beat his wife,
which is no way to court
another woman, and I
just got fat and
ballooned out of her life.
Dear Betsy still sweet
and somewhere in Smithers.

DULCE (this dulse) *ET DECORUM*   /57

In the luminous Pacific blue we rode
lightly in your brother's sloop
and I didn't mind your shaggy pubic
hair, nor did he.   But his prissy
pommy friend, an editor at *Reader's*
Digest, seemed awkward all day.
None of us were naked, exactly,
but what jungles you bequeathed
upon our deck   great hairy bushes
filled with carnivorous blooms.

I liked the danger of your foliage
even more than the sharks in
the broad river mouth.   Then back
to Sydney harbour on a stiff twilight
breeze, your rug calling out to
its seadrift kin: rockweed,
dulse and kelp.

FOR CHRISTINE THE JAZZ GROUPIE I LOVED   /58

I wept on schedule for my kids and you also wept
troubled by your typing classes. When we made love
coming seemed to pierce you like a burning spear.
But you were fond of me and I of you, and together
we saw many foreign films, had myriad curried meals,
wrote poems, and once sailed across Sydney harbour
in your brother's boat.   Why didn't we stay to-
gether? It would have been grand, as crazy as you
were, as much as I grieved for my children — and
the way you collected oddities, having slept with
jazzmen of renown, having fist-fucked an admiral's
son from Virginia.   Surely I was tame and rather
tepid.   But when I left, there was no glass uni-
corn to break. And the Chinese poem you brushed
in loving farewell — for all its mistakes —
was as beautiful as you.

NOVENA FOR GRACE KELLY /59

So there's poor Raymond Burr standing in the darkened doorway
and Jimmy Stewart sitting cold and quiet, though really scared
shitless — What do you want? Thorwald says, Money? I have
none. But Jimmy's got Grace Kelly and what more could you want?
No one ever looked as beautiful as her in *Rear Window,* and even
now with her precious bones resting in state, with thin grim men
weeping calmly over her grave, we still remember her. This novena
is especially for her — for the most stunning profile this
side of Eve.

How many times have I seen that picture? That perfect
jawline running exquisitely up to her ear, the consummate tilt
of her pert little nose? Poor Thorwald had no money, and Raymond
Burr, the dignified Canuck, never got a chance to make love to
Gracy. Somehow he stands for all overweight lunkheads, tied to
nagging harpies around the world. He's the existential hero
of Western cinema. The loud broad always making fun of his suit,
throwing dinner in his boring face, the chops he'd spent hours
on, complete with plastic tulip. As if she could do better: on
her butt all day while Thorwald's out hustling cheap baubles.
No one ever told him life was like this — he should never have
left the farm in Matsqui. Just a few scrubby acres, but at
least he'd have some self-respect. Even now, with Grace
just dust in a jar.

FROM THE CAULDRON

FROM THE ABYSMAL CAULDRON

O these things from the depths, caught with
n(y)ets of Russian thistle: a pea shooter full
of lead; a coin with two heads and one tail;
cabbage at fire sale prices; a recipe for cos-
mic confederation; the secret location of the
much coveted arc; rose-hip tea bags with love
handles; a conversation course in Spanish for
lovers and other herbivores; and words with-
out homes to go to, words on the lamb, words
without candles or novenas, words trembling
like panthers in equatorial heat — words,
realities, caught from the cauldron.

SO FRIGGIN' BLUE

It's funny for awhile, then not so funny, then downright
fucking blue.   You say the phases of a biochemical
moon run through our blood!   Maybe, but last night in
the tub I had to put down the book I was reading —
peeping from the back of my head was a diamond light
bigger'n your fist.   *O Bliss!* I sang, breathin' deep
through my nose, then chanting   *OM MANI PADME HUM!*
OH MOMMA, MOMMA PLEASE COME HOME!

Having a cold, my septum made a noise like an oboe,
so I played myself for awhile, then took to begging
this sweet light to stay (which it didn't)   and the
bath cooled off and I thought of my friends in
Vancouver.   My lover on the streets — how she
won't come home.   Then I wept and wept
so friggin' blue.

DIAPHANEITY, THE VISIBLE ORIGINS   /63

Driven from the house by the mindless joy of
someone else's kids,   I escape to the garden:
the little patch of green I call Paradise.
Hasn't my wife done a nice job? I hear
myself cooing to the pigeons next door:
daisies, portulaca, daffodils and glads.
It's nice enough,   if you don't mind the
wires overhead: Presenting *The Garden*,
by Sask Power and Piet Mondrian.

But the dogs in the alley are barking boors
and the trucks and lawnmowers never stop.
Only in the shed is there quiet enough,
for Pissarro's *Garden With Trees in Blossom,
Spring, Pontoise* — where stillness
endows on its new white petals   a clear
light breaking free from the ground.

FROGS AND WASPS /64

Onion Lake.   Spring.   20 below.
Red ice on morning lagoon.
Country in peril.   Frogs
and wasps.   Life on the pond
is violent.   Stick to flies,
froggy   stick to butterflies.
Wasps   on the other hand,
steal favours from their royal
cousins, the bees.   They are
only good for malice and the
raping of plums.

At Onion Lake the sweetgrass
grows thin and gold in winter.
The honey pond takes all
the shit we can give it.
The beavers no longer eager,
the country tired.

OREGON RAIN   /65

Rain in Oregon, I suppose
and up the coast to Saltspring Island.
Soft grey rain   muted horns of liquid
unrequited love.   Clearing the
Rockies   down to flat golden prairie,
the hungry soul dreams diamond heart
in crinoline — 300 million eyes
endlessly searching this real estate.
Longing, musing: how many
        could I ever love, even
                with a bevy of lives?

THE POET AND FRIENDS (4) /66

Three wordsmiths are lonely tonight, two boys
and a girl. Two of them were married once, and now
they're not, though one would like another try
and the other hangs on to a branch within reach.
They enact a series of simple plays:
1. falling in love with someone who'll never love you back.
2. wanting to make up with your ex-wife.
3. wanting nobody for a long time, or at least pretending.
4. wanting a nice warm body on a cold winter night.
5. being nicer than you really are to win a special heart.
There are many more of these. Or is there basically only
one? The heart can die with a single thought. But I wish
them well, all so deserving of whatever they need. And who
now ride briskly through this prairie town, or walk by the
river with their bags of heavy books — they'll soon be
writing better poems than ever. And it's what they want
more than anything: eros in the mouth, words
spilling over the brilliant page.

ANIKO/ONE   /67

I don't think I've ever told you why I like Greek food wrapped
in vine leaves, she said, and we said, no, you haven't. Well,
it was long ago when I was just a girl, she continued, in her
polished apple way, and we pulled up mugs of tea to the picnic
table, lit pipes and smiled, our minds roaming back to before
the Second World War. I was not quite sixteen, and went down to
London to visit my sister and her boyfriend, Kurt, the German-
Jew — I felt very pleased with myself, for all the reasons girls
do when they're almost sixteen and travelling alone in the big
safe world. They were marvelous hosts, and took me to Soho to a
Greek place where Kurt fell almost immediately in love with me.
And my sister, who had many boyfriends, and was engaged fifteen
times before she finally married, went upstairs to find a bath-
room. Finding a long queue of young women, she went to the end
of the line to await her turn. But it wasn't a line for the bath-
room after all — it was a recruitment station for whores
bound for South America.

Well, my sister laughed so hard she couldn't pee, and came down
stairs in rollicking agony. Soon we were all laughing together
and made our way out of the cafe where, much to our surprise, the
Maltese chef was stabbed to death right before our eyes. Another
Maltese came running up behind him and stabbed him in the back —
swoosh, right through the heart. It was the first murder I ever
witnessed and I was understandably shaken — but it was also the

beginning of a most marvelous affair, and even better because Kurt sent me books. I remember getting *Howard's End,* by Forster, and being very pleased as it was one of the first Penguin paperbacks. Kurt eventually went back to Germany, and I think he must have died there during the war. So, whenever I eat anything rolled up in vine leaves, I think fondly of him — savouring the foliage of our sweet green love.

ANIKO/TWO

Most writers out here write into
the landscape, she said, peering
into her goldfish pond. I write
out of it — which makes sense
when you think about it. She's
the only grandmother in town
reading Cosmology and the New
Physics. I'm really a Blakean,
you know, she muttered one day,
ladling out ratatouille — *the
body is the emanation of the soul.*
Eternity is always now.

ANIKO/THREE

When she was very young and couldn't see well
at all, the world was a magical blurry place,
full of bright rainbows like coloured tree-lights
at Christmas. So when her fine avuncular uncle
called one time with a gift of gold-rimmed specs,
she was grateful at first, but soon felt the loss.

Rainbows were only little coloured bulbs after all,
and the mystical streams and currents only everyday
kinds of things. Once, all she could see clearly
were the plants she knelt before with her brother
in the woods. Birds are too fast for you, he'd said,
but plants hardly ever fly away.

Now she'd learn to read and write, and someday become
a famous poet. But the magic never returned, or at
least not until years later, when she'd married for
love and gone west to the prairies. In Saskatchewan,
she said, the magic came back — came roaring to life
in the blur of the distance.

ANIKO/FOUR   /71

When driving on the hot summer prairie, she said, you used
to come to these old cafes - all pretty much the same, all
painted bilious green, with high ceilings and big rotating
fans. You'd pile in and order pie and coke, and the heat
inside was every bit as bad as the hell you'd just driven
through. There was even a joke about drivers on the
prairies — how their arms came off with the doors. But
it was the only way to keep cool out there, hanging out
the window catching every little breeze.

There's nothing like driving on those far southern flats,
she continued. While the heat seems to put your body to
sleep, your mind climbs up a shimmering blue sky. *The most
spiritual landscape in the world.*

THE PRACTICE OF DEPTH   /72

She said *dabbling in Aristotle would make a fine title for a
book*, and I thought hhhmmmnnnnn, just like a woman — or just
like this woman, to be exact. Baby, when will you learn how
to flow. What we thought was arthritis is just the long-term
effect of your much-too-editorial mind. Now the Presocratics,
that's another matter — *dabbling in the Presocratics*, what a
fine and impossible thing. Why you can't just dabble in all
that ontological gas — it's quicksand! It's the primordial
stuff! One spark and you're up in flames.

I've been burnt a few times, so I know what I'm talking about.
Walking around Smithers and Telkwa with a mind full of roaring
butterflies, having all my projects devoured by a calico sky —
it's the new consciousness, girl, and there's nothing new under
the moon. Now take Heraclitus, for in/stance: how're you go-
ing to make it with a cat who buries himself in a dung pile?
In all your precious years throwing back mint juleps, you
never once was asked to dig shit. How offal, you would have
cried, holding a nose-gay of poems to your delicate muzzle.

A NEW SLANT ON EXTINCTION   /73

Some of these giants were pacifists and would have worn long hair
and played guitars and zithers. The Brontosaurus, for example,
knew all mantras from the beginning of time. While munching on
hay and alfalfa, this peaceful Pastor of the rushes would enact
the strains of Creation — there'd be a colossal BBBAAANNNNGGGG!
as the brute would slap its monstrous tail on the surface of a
pond — smaller more receptive lizards would close their lidded
peepers and, in the back of their primordial minds, stars would
form out of molten light. The terrible lizards were mystics,
you see. Only Tyrannosaurus Rex had analytical skills; his teeth
were like buttons on a cash register. Tearing flesh with preci-
sion and joy, they tabulated the take like ambitious bankers.

Dinosaurs in the last days, confronting extinction. Living out
their wildest fantasies, existential dinos meditated upon the
death of their species. Some proclaimed dino heavens and escha-
tologies, handing out pamphlets and irritating everyone with
their inane and idiot smiles. But they all scrambled for codes,
for acts of penance and meaning — only T. Rex got stuck in the
concrete, wanting to take it all with him, hoarding carrion in
heaps, stockpiling more than could be eaten. Let the market lead
the way, he grimaced, as his children were stolen and eaten by
rodents. The ultimate merger rotted in his mind like Hadrosaur
chops in the desert sun. What would you do at the end of time.

FLIGHT   /74

Before midnight and under solemn autumn sky,
with coyotes yapping by trout-stocked slough,
there came signs overhead of chthonic navigation:
wild cranes, wild geese full of ripened grain —

And there arrived in dream a man with two caps:
one with wings, another with gills; and I dreamt
of oceans full of fulgent stars, and woke be-
holding light in my ripening mind.

BEDTIME GNOSIS

Lying with my little boy
one night   I thought
how like a hand
in a stocking of silk
imagination
explores
the unknown.

IT IS CLEAR   /76

It's clear that Gavin descending the basement
stairs while I read from Yeats is a meaning
complete in itself. With his fair skin and
starlight eyes, with his stocky build and
lovely bare feet on the wood, he's more than
enough for this or any lifetime. What more
can I know than this sensible confluence
of beauty? This child I love, this music
bespeaking my heart — *In my golden house
on high,* says Mr. Yeats, *There
they shine eternally.*

GAVIN'S FEET: THE PERILS OF NEGATIVE THEOLOGY   /77

Gavin comes down the blue wooden stairs
with old black sweat pants rolled up
to reveal his calves. Slowly, with a thump,
his small bare feet hit the steps. Slowly
the pale translucent flesh of his legs
descends before my eyes — as I sit
in the basement at my desk, pulling my
beard and dreaming of God.

God is everywhere and nowhere, someone
once said. If so, how can he remember
all the names of the damned? How
can he notice every feather of every
skylark eaten by every cat? I
feel comfortable in this knowledge, that
God is everywhere and nowhere. At least
half the time I'm in the clear.

THE FINGER STEEPLE POINTING

I don't understand the difference:
some golden   covered in pollen,
but others seem glazed for the oven.
Two cities?   Or steps on a ladder?

I want to be with the dusty ones:
quiet   in the heart of things,
humble   in the presence of death.
That walking white heat where
humour's distilled   leaving
nothing but permanent smiles.

Leaving soul pollen   golden
on some animal's back: a
retriever chasing trees
or pissing at the wind.
Shit, I don't know!   Who does?
Who knows where *soul stuff* abideth?
The finger only a steeple pointing.

OH, THE WONDER

/79

Oh, the wonder of these beautiful animals that love to dress
in skins of silk and gold, and are suns, each in their own time, diamonds
spinning through cosmic reaches — and I love them, watch them
dancing, singing, loving, ripping their wondrous hides in frenzied
passion, mirrors to one another — men and women, wrapped in the
language of evolving gods, their intercourse crashing like thunder,
lightning, windroaring. And the tumultuous climb to the One is
ecstasy, and they hunger for it above all else, enduring all severities,
making mockery of existence, sleeping, then waking with the blood
fury peculiar to their doomed species . . . Omnivorous like their gods,
they drink straight from the vein, then polish their cups for the altar.

And the wonder of these creatures is the perilous nature of
their minds, for they skate helplessly over an intricate blackness, silver
blades crisscrossing the delicate ice — and they know nothing other than
skating . . . these poor animals, these comfort seeking vertebrates, they
are born with silver knives tied to their tender soles . . . tottering under
a midnight sky they come to awareness, stars blazing, mist rolling
down through oak groves and cedar. No wonder they're terrified!
Swirling the length of their insignificant lives. But life is like that, and
sex too: sweetest on thinnest ice.

Pain blossoms into the vault, withers quickly, then dies; though
visions of Eternity sweeten everything, no one wants to say good-
bye . . . even the Garden of Gethsemane, where Christ didn't want
to leave his friends, making promises He wasn't sure He could keep,
anything to soothe their aching hearts . . . FOR GOD SO LOVED
THE WORLD . . . He told them tales to keep them off the streets and
out of trouble; stories full of glorious angels beckoning from the wings,
ladders leading eternally upward, harmonious spheres rippling golden

/80

tones through the ripping pain of existence! SEEK AND YE SHALL FIND, KNOCK AND THE DOOR SHALL OPEN!

And when these poor servants lay their bodies down for the night, they mumble faint prayers and tug quietly at their gowns, for even beings drawn largely from water have some sense of decorum . . . animals as aqueous as fishbowls, pouring down their aquiferous bones in the dark, gargling their horizontal declarations of love, both male and female in this cozy aquacade . . . But when asleep they dream of being great Blue Whales, lovers bigger than the idea of death . . . O SWIRLING DRAIN AT THE BOTTOM OF THE FOUNTAIN! O TERROR OF THE DEEP! . . . then they cling tightly one-to-the-other with cries of "BABY, BABY, BABY!" Plugging up the drains where the juice runs out . . . plunging and plugging, huffing and puffing, surfacing covered with algae and smiles . . . THERE SHE BLOWS! . . . Spouting off ecstatically, quivering meat covered with silken organ called skin, tongues licking salty sweat and semen, lips drinking primordial seas, gulping, gargling, gasping for air . . . "YES, BABY, YES! THIS IS THE WAY TO PARADISE!" Taboo versions of synchronized swimming.

Then tired, finally, from bawdy love . . . crawling slowly up the mind's sandy shelves . . . they discover they have arms again, the dream of whaling over. They reach for tobacco and booze like water reaching for fire: very elemental. Inhaling deeply the smoke, pondering their shattered bliss, they wash out slowly on the tide, drowning into sleep. Having fucked away the emptiness they are void, like water dribbling from a cheap trick glass. For when they drown, these phantoms drawn chiefly from ocean . . . when their air/sacs fill with H_2O, their eyes lose the lustre of the diamond within. And when they drown in those pearly seas, hungering for mermaid angels and a father named Poseidon, they finally give their bodies to the element called home . . . all sojourns in air must lead to this.